How to Become a Pharmacy Technician

How I became a Pharmacy Tech in 90 Days

For Less than $500

BY

REBECCA WILDER

CSB Academy Publishing Co.
P. O. Box 966
Semmes, Alabama 36575, USA

Cover designed by
Angie Anderson

First Edition

TABLE OF CONTENTS

INTRODUCTION

If you are reading this book, it means you are seriously considering a career as a pharmacy technician. There are many good reasons to get started, from the hours to job stability. I can say based on my personal experience; it was one of the best decisions I ever made.

WHY I BECAME A PHARMACY TECHNICIAN

When I finished high school, I really didn't have a plan for my life. College wasn't something that I felt was right for me because I had no idea what I would want to do. With the high cost of tuition, I didn't want to end up going into serious debt just for a piece of paper that would earn me only slightly more than my high school degree. Many of my friends went to college, and most of them did not finish. The one who did were earning less than I was after they graduated.

I wasn't earning a fortune but did have a steady 45 to 50 hours a week at $9 an hour. With two daughters, it was just enough to get by. We didn't have anything extra, but we were able to pay all of the bills.

Then I got laid off.

The company had decided to outsource all of the jobs to Asia, and we were given a week's notice. Since we were hourly, we didn't get severance.

At first, I was in shock. I had not earned enough to save much really, and there weren't many jobs. I began thinking I should have gone to college because now my friends were earning more than I could. Still, they owed a lot on their student loans.

So how was I going to make ends meet?

Around that time, one of my daughters got sick. When I went to the pharmacy to pick up her prescription, I mentioned my situation to the pharmacist. She told me she wasn't actually a pharmacist, but a pharmacist technician. We talked for a bit, and I found out that it wasn't nearly as impossible as the job sounded. My previous job, working in customer support, actually gave me many of the basic skills I would need.

When I told her that I didn't have a lot of extra money and that the only job I could find paid minimum wage, she told me it wasn't necessary to go to school. The only required expense was for the certification exam.

Having gone into the pharmacy dreading another cost we couldn't afford, I walked out feeling that I had found something that could be exactly what I needed.

It was such a freeing experience that I wanted to let others know that they too have options. You don't have to stick with a job you don't like. Being a pharmacy technician is both challenging and rewarding. I also love that I get to have more time with my daughters because the hours are more flexible.

SO WHAT IS A PHARMACY TECHNICIAN?

Like pharmacists, pharmacist technicians work in a number of different environments, including grocery stores, dedicated pharmacies, and hospitals. Each of the different locations has different levels of stability, different pay rates, and their own schedules.

Pharmacy technicians are largely responsible for helping customers. From talking to them and scheduling a time to talk to the pharmacist to taking payments, I spend a lot of time helping people. I do work with the compounds, mostly taking measurements and filling prescriptions.

Since I talk to the clients, I can actually see how the medication is helping, which is one of the things I love best about the job. Knowing that I am making a difference and helping people heal is far more rewarding than any of the other jobs I have held.

The Primary Responsibilities of a Pharmacy Technician

Their primary job is to assist licensed pharmacist. While they are not qualified to actually fill the prescriptions from health professionals and customers, there are a number of practical tasks that technicians perform.

- Use information from the pharmacist to measure out the necessary ingredients for a prescription.
- Prepare the packaging and labeling of the prescriptions.
- Organize and maintain the inventory, alerting the pharmacist when a particular supply or ingredient is running low.

The majority of a pharmacy technician's tasks involve working with customers. These tasks include taking the initial information about a prescription that needs to be filled, setting up time for customers to talk to the pharmacist, answering phone calls, and handling payments and the insurance claims process.

CURRENT REGULATIONS

The federal government has not established a set of rules and guidelines to govern this particular field. Instead, every state has its own rules and regulations that address how much a technician can do, and the minimum requirements before someone qualifies to fill this role. In some states, pharmacist technicians are allowed to mix compounds as long as they are supervised by a licensed pharmacist. In hospitals, pharmacy technicians may even be responsible for dispensing medications to the patients.

A ROSY FUTURE

According to the US Department of Labor, the outlook for this particular career is expected to rise 20% between 2012 and 2022, considerably faster than most other professions. There are a number of reasons why pharmacy technicians are in rising demand, including an increasingly aging population and the fact that more people have insurance to cover medical needs.

Because the requirements to become a technician are easier to meet, it is a great way to get into a steady, growing profession. If you are interested in learning more about the requirements in your state, the National Association of Boards of Pharmacy has posted information by state on their website.

TWO APPROACHES

There are two different ways to approach the exam that is required by a majority of states.

If you prefer a more traditional learning environment, there are a number of online resources, vocational schools, and community colleges that can help you plan and prepare for the test. You need to know how much you will need to spend and how much time you have to complete them. This will give you the guidance you need to plan your next move and start to schedule your time around the exam date.

There are adequate resources online for those who either do not learn well in a more traditional learning environment or who do not have the time or the money to work based on someone else's timeline. If you want to be able to take the test in less than a month (something that you won't be able to do through most of the paid resources), you can dedicate a lot of time and energy into studying. This gives you more control over your timeline and the cost.

I can honestly say that either way works. I currently work with several pharmacy technicians, and about half of us passed by studying on our own. However, the people who took classes tended to pass on the first round, while those of us who studied on our own usually took two tries.

MY APPROACH

What most people don't realize is that you don't have to take classes to become a pharmacy technician. I didn't have the time or money to go to school. I earned my certification through hard work and constantly studying.

Once I learned about pharmacy technicians, I spent the next month studying. It was hard work. At the time, I had two jobs that paid minimum wage, and I was studying for the pharmacy technician exam during what little time I had available. I also made sure to understand the rules and regulations for Alabama since every state has its own requirements.

I studied an hour or two every day for that month. The week before my scheduled exam, I started taking practice exams at least once a day. My daughters would actually come in and ask me questions too, so we all worked together. I also took the time to find out what I had to do to prepare for the exam, like what kinds of identification to bring.

Since I didn't have any extra money, the only cost I paid was for the exam itself. There are many websites that offer assistance free of charge, and I used as many as I could find.

I have to admit; I was incredibly nervous when I went in. Several of the people taking it were on their second or third try, which I found out was pretty common. I think this made me a little less nervous because I knew that I would be able to retake the test if I didn't pass. This was only the first out of three tries.

It was hard work, but I found out as soon as the test was over that I had passed. Even better, I only missed a few problems, which made me feel pretty proud.

After passing my test, I applied to work in one of the hospitals. While the days tend to be longer, I only work four days a week, and I am earning far more than I was at the job where I was laid off. Even better, I now have time to spend with my daughters. My youngest is even considering becoming a pharmacy technician.

THE EXAM

The exam does have an associated cost, as well as a restriction on the number of times you can take it before you have to pass. If you choose to pay for courses and classes, the cost of the exam may be included. If you plan to go it alone, you will need to plan to save up for the cost of the exam when you apply to take it.

IS IT THE RIGHT PATH FOR YOU?

Everyone is different. Here are a few questions that can help you decide if this is the right path for you.

- Are you having trouble finding a job?
- Do you feel your life has gone off course?
- Are you unsure what to do for a career?
- Can you spare some time to study a little every day?
- Do you like helping people?
- Do you want more out of your job than just a paycheck?
- Would you like to have more flexible hours?
- Do you feel like your job is going nowhere?
- Are you concerned about cutbacks and being laid off?

If you answered yes to any of these questions, becoming a pharmacy technician is a great career to look into. Odds are you will love it as much as I do.

This book is designed to help you determine if you think that being a pharmacy technician is what lies in your future. I give you the information you need to understand what it is and how you can benefit from it. Because it is not regulated by a single entity (like the federal government), I also give you the tools you need to help you understand the applicable rules and regulations for each state.

Remember every state has different guidelines and requirements, so you will need to do some of your own research to make sure you cover your bases. This book is based on my personal experience, and I live in Alabama. However, the test is standardized, so the same resources should be helpful, regardless of what state you live in.

Chapter 10 gives you a number of useful resources to help you succeed, no matter what path you choose.

In this book, I am trying to give you everything you need to determine if it is the career for you, and if so, what you can do to get started today.

CHAPTER 1. WHY SHOULD I CONSIDER BECOMING A PHARMACY TECHNICIAN?

There are a lot of very good reasons why becoming a pharmacy technician is a great idea. The following are some of the main benefits that you should consider if you are thinking about making a career in this profession.

- Steady income
- Ability to advance your career
- Shorter work weeks
- Job satisfaction

If you want a real career that does not require going into serious debt with student loans and that can be extremely rewarding, you should seriously consider becoming a pharmacy technician.

It certainly isn't as glamorous as becoming a doctor, but it doesn't require you to spend eight years in school either. It may not be as prestigious as being a nurse, but it is far less stressful.

If you are seriously becoming a pharmacist, but don't know what the job entails or want to get a closer look before making your decision, becoming a technician first can help. It gives you hands-on experience in the field. The experience also lets you see exactly what being a pharmacist entails so you can determine if it is the right path for you.

You may even find that being a pharmacy technician is enough in its own right. It is a respectable position with great benefits.

SALARY

According to the US Bureau of Labor Statistics, pharmacy technicians averaged close to $30,000 a year in 2012. There were three factors that played into how much a person earned in the position:

- Years of experience
- Location of residence
- Type of pharmacy where the technician worked

The first two factors are typical factors for any career. The more experience you have, the more earning potential you have. And people who live in large cities almost always earn more than people who live in rural areas because it is more expensive to live in a cit. While $30,000 may not be enough to live in a place like New York City, it is more than adequate for a smaller town in most of the country.

LOCATIONS THAT PAY THE BEST

Different cities in California tend to be the highest paying locations, such as Oakland, Napa, and San Francisco. The following California cities saw pharmacy technicians earn over $45,000 on average during 2013.

- Oakland had the highest average earnings at $49,950.
- Napa came in a close second, with the average pharmacy technician earning over $46,000 a year.
- San Francisco, San Jose, and Madera had nearly the same earning potential on average at $45,790, $45,280, and $45,280, respectively.

However, California also has a much higher standard of living that most other states. Before moving, make sure the salary potential matches how much it will cost to live in the location. You may find that you can make your salary go further by staying in your current location.

TOP SALARY

The top 10% of pharmacy technicians earned over $40,000 in 2012. The best-paid people in the field earned nearly $45,000 in 2013. When you consider that this career does not require you to work five days a week, that can translate to more free time.

TYPE OF PHARMACY

The best paying pharmacy technician positions were those held by federal employees. On average they earned $40,890 a year. The top five paying positions in the private sector in 2012 were as follows:

- Ambulatory health care services at over $35,000 a year
- Hospitals (including private, state, and locally run) at over $33,500 a year
- Grocery stores and drug stores at $28,760 and $28,030, respectively, a year
- General merchandise stores at over just over $27,000 a year

Your hours will vary based on which kind of pharmacy you work in, so some of these positions include working later hours or weekends.

Over half of all pharmacy technicians work in a drug store pharmacy. The next highest percentage of pharmacy technicians worked in hospitals.

STABILITY

This field is not only incredibly stable; it is in growing demand. As people live longer, they need more medications. This means that pharmacies need more people to help work in them, and most of them do not want to pay for a lot of pharmacists. This means that you are going to be in a field that is growing more rapidly than most other professions. There is a very good chance that as the demand grows, those who are already experienced will see their salary increase more rapidly.

This is the ideal time to be getting into the profession because businesses are starting to realize the need, but haven't been as quick to respond. Once they do, it will mean you will have a greater selection of where you want to work, whether in a different city, state, or just a different facility.

Because it is in demand, you are also more likely to find a job quickly if you decide to relocate. For people who like to move around with some frequency, this is a great job to have. You get the best of both worlds: job stability and the opportunity to move when you want.

CAREER ADVANCEMENT

Pharmacy technicians are in a unique position to learn about a number of different fields, not just about pharmacies. As you interact with doctors' offices, you have the chance to talk to people of a similar position to learn more about what other technicians do. If you are fortunate enough to work in a hospital, you can talk to people in different positions and specialties to see if any of them are the kind you think you could do.

If you find that working in a pharmacy is something that you enjoy, you can look into becoming a full-time pharmacist down the road. It will mean more schooling and education, but you will already have some experience, as well as people who can help you with your studies.

LENGTH OF THE AVERAGE WORK WEEK

Pharmacies are one of the few professions that still keep a more regulated schedule. When you go to the grocery store, you have probably noticed that the pharmacy is closed long before most of the other area.

Depending on where you work, you may be able to have a schedule that is only three or four days a week. This is a great way to earn extra money if you don't want a full-time job. It is also an ideal set up if you decide to go for a degree that will help you become a pharmacist as you will have more time for schooling and studying.

A REWARDING EXPERIENCE

There are few careers outside of the medical profession that offer the kinds of rewards you get in the medical profession, including pharmacy technicians.

A REAL CAREER

It is a real career that can have a relatively flexible schedule. You will learn basic skills to help you either progress in this field or move to one that you find more intriguing.

FINANCIAL BENEFITS

Because it is incredibly stable, you will be able to start getting your finances in order. This is something that has become increasingly difficult to find, and one of the primary benefits of becoming a pharmacy technician. Because you won't have four years of student loans when you finish, you will be able to start putting away more of your salary for retirement or toward other financial goals, like buying a house.

MAKING A DIFFERENT – JOB SATISFACTION

This is likely the more important benefit. You will get to watch people recover on a regular basis, giving you a real sense of accomplishment in your everyday work. Customers may come up to the window to thank you for what you have done to help them recover. As you watch children and adults alike recover from various illnesses, you will know that you played an important role in their recovery. In terms of job satisfaction, there are very few that can offer the kind of reward that you get by knowing that what you do makes a real difference in people's lives. Being a pharmacy technician gives you this kind of job satisfaction, and you get to see the positive effects on a regular basis.

CHAPTER 2. WHAT SKILLS ARE REQUIRED?

The necessary skills and education to become a pharmacy technician are far more lenient than most other technician positions, such as radiological or dental hygienist technicians. With roughly 355,300 in this position during 2012, there is a growing need for more in the different pharmaceutical environments.

One thing you should know is that every state has a different set of regulations and requirement on what is necessary to become a pharmacy technician. This book presents general guidelines for what is necessary. Refer to Chapter 7 for more information and links to help you get the information you need about this career path in your state.

You will also need to pass the Board Examinations. This is covered in Chapter 5.

MINIMUM EDUCATION REQUIREMENTS

Regardless of where you live within the United States, you have to have at least a high school education to become a pharmacy technician. You can either earn a high school diploma or get your GED to meet this requirement.

The majority of your actual learning will be on the job, although there are some postsecondary programs that you should look into for a boost in salary.

Some states will require you to have additional education, certification, or licenses. Make sure you know what is required in your state.

NECESSARY SKILLS

The primary job of the pharmacy technician is to deal with the customers. As a unique type of customer support, it is essential that people develop several social skills:

- Pharmacy technicians have to be able to interact with customers and be helpful. Keeping in mind that many of the people you deal with feel ill, you should expect that they will not be at their best. This means you need to be patient and understanding.
- Coupled with the ability to deal with your customers, you have to be able to listen to them. If someone tells you that they are allergic to a particular type of medication, you need to make sure the pharmacist is aware before the medication is provided.
- You need to develop skills that help you to be detail oriented. The people you are dealing with on a daily basis are sick and may have serious health problems. This means you need to be aware of restrictions and problems. It may be the pharmacist's job to make sure the right

medication is made, but you should be there to help avoided any complications. A great

- Organizational skill is absolutely necessary. You cannot properly handle your customers if you have a cluttered front area. Data needs to be entered into the database as soon as possible, and files need to be kept for things like audits and reviews. You will have a number of different responsibilities, so you will need to be able to work with both the pharmacists and the customers. This means being able to find what you need when you need it.
- The last skill you need is math. You won't have to know how to work with the more complex maths, like calculus, but you will need at least basic math skills. Some pharmacies allow technicians to measure out compounds, and you will need to be able to count the pills to meet the needs for the amount of time specified by the pharmacist.

The position may be primarily focused on the customers, but you will spend a considerable amount of time interacting with the pharmacist. This means you will likely be required to relay information from time to time. Developing basic communication and math skills will go a very long way to making you successful as a pharmacy technician.

MOVING FORWARD

You can choose one of the several different paths to get started. If you are satisfied with your high school education and feel that the next best step for you is on the job training, many employers offer on the job training. Each employer will have a different set up for how you are trained and the amount of information that you need to know.

Either way, you will likely need to pass the Board of Examination.

GOING BACK TO SCHOOL

There are a number of schools that provide certification for a year or less of education. Frequently, vocational and community colleges can give you what you need with a minimum amount of schooling. If you would like additional time, some schools offer an associate's degree in for this particular field.

STUDYING ON YOUR OWN

If you do not feel you have the time or funds to go back to school, you can study for the Board Examinations on your own. This will require a good bit of time and self-discipline on your part. Chapter 6 covers more details about what you need to know. If you think this is the right path for you, the chapter can help you get focused on the right programs and information that you need to pass the test.

WARNING ABOUT DIFFERENT STATE LAWS

Every state has the right to determine what the minimum requirements are for this particular position. This is the case because different states allow for different responsibilities to be given to pharmacy technicians. Some states require certification or licensing before you can be hired.

Even in states where it isn't a requirement, there are employers who are willing to cover the cost for their employees to take the exam. It is an investment that can pay off in the long run as it gives the employers staff who are more familiar with what needs to be done. It also means that the technicians can provide greater assistance to the main pharmacists.

PASSING THE BOARD EXAMINATIONS

Chapter 5 provides details about the Board Examinations. While there are two certifications, most states only require the first.

- The Pharmacy Technician Certification Board offers certification to those who have a high school diploma and pass the Board Examinations.
- The National Health Career Association certification requires participants to be at least 18 years old and completed high school to take the example. They must also have been through

a training program or completed a year in the field to qualify.

Neither of these tests is particularly difficult. Most people start with the Pharmacy Technician Certification because it has less strict requirements.

What you should know is that when people talk about the Board Examinations, they primarily mean the one offered by the PTCB. Five different organizations have worked together to create a national standard to help guide states since the federal government has not created any guidelines for this specific position.

This does not mean that there are not federal regulations that you need to be concerned with when you take the exam. It simply means that the federal regulations are about pharmacy and medications, which are still very much relevant to the technicians. All applicable federal regulations that govern what you need to know to work in the pharmacy industry are included in what you learn to pass the test.

What this means for you is that you won't have to research sources and regulations covered by several different types of government. The test has been standardized so that all federal laws are covered by the exam.

Most states look to the exam for guidance as well. These states have made passing the certification exam a requirement for those seeking to be pharmacy technicians.

Later chapters will cover more information on these aspects of the exams. For now, you just need to know that primary exam to prepare for is the certification offered by the PTCB.

CHAPTER 3. WILL I NEED TO GO TO SCHOOL TO GET A JOB?

In most cases, you will not have to go to school to be qualified for the position. However, most states (or in some cases employers) do strongly recommend or require certification.

If you are thinking about becoming a pharmacy technician, you will have to have at least a high school level education, whether you get a diploma or a GED.

To find out if you will need further education to become a pharmacy technician, consult the Pharmacy Technician Career Guide. It will give you details on what is required for each state. Some states have pretty strict requirements, such as certification and hands on experience. Other states give preference to candidates who earned the certification, but it isn't required.

To give you an idea of how diverse the requirements are here is a quick look at a couple of states.

- Alabama requires that you have a job with a pharmacy first. Then you have to get certified and register with the state board.
- California, the state where pharmacy technicians have the most earning potential, has the most rigid requirements, but there are

a number of ways to qualify for a position. You must meet one of the following conditions to be considered as a viable candidate for any pharmacy in California.

  - You must earn an associate's degree in pharmacy technology.
  - The courses you take have to earn you at least 240 hours of hands-on training. Alternatively, you can complete the ASHP training courses.

- Colorado doesn't have any requirements. This means you don't have to be certified or licensed. However, those who have either earned the certification or have had additional education, are more likely to land a job at the entry level.
- Louisiana requires nearly as much work as California. Like Alabama, it has steps you must complete before you are considered. You will need to complete the steps in the following order.
  - You must be employed at a pharmacy.
  - You must apply for the Pharmacy Technician Candidate certification through the state board.
  - Once you are certified, you are required to complete a state-approved training program. You will have one and a half years after your certification to complete the training. In this time, you must complete 600 hours of practical experience. Of that time, 200 hours must be done through the training program.

- Finally, you have to pass the board approved certification exam.

- New York state has no applicable regulations to be a licensed pharmacy technician.
- Wyoming requires pharmacy technicians to have a PTCB certification.

The majority of states require some level of certification or experience. Make sure you look into what is required for your state before you start looking into classes. In most cases, additional training or certification will help you get your foot in the door.

Whether you are looking to get into pharmacy technician as a degree or if you are planning to move and need to see what guidelines you have to follow, this website is incredibly helpful in planning your next move on a state-by-state basis. Most states require either Pharmacy Technician Certification Board (also called PTCB) certification or completion of a program that is accredited by the American Society of Health-System Pharmacists.

CONTINUING YOUR EDUCATION

This is a career designed for people who are not certain what they want to do or do not have the time or the money to attend a full-time university for four years. That is why the vast majority of pharmacy technicians who seek additional education attend either a community college or a vocational school.

SHORT PATH

Because the courses are largely designed to help you get your certification, it will take you a year or less to complete the program. They help to guide you through all of the necessary areas of the exam that you need to pass. Some schools include the cost of the exam as part of the tuition, so make sure you ask before committing to the courses. You want to know if you will need to save additional money for the exam. If a school does not cover the cost of the exam, do some research into the other schools in your area to see if they do.

GETTING AN ASSOCIATES

If you are more interested in getting a degree as part of your additional education, there are some schools that offer an associate's degree for taking two years' worth of courses. You will learn more about the job, what a pharmacist does, and may be able to start at a higher salary than those who only aim to get the certification.

Like the program that takes a year or less, make sure you check to see if the cost of the degree includes certification. You may be able to go for the National Health Career Association certification after getting an associate's degree.

RELEVANT COURSEWORK

The primary focus of schooling is to help you prepare for dealing with customers and offering support to the pharmacists. Most of the course work focuses on the tasks you will need to do. The following are the areas that most programs, both the certification and the associate's degree, cover.

- Basic mathematics, particularly arithmetic
- Recordkeeping
- How medications are dispensed
- The laws and ethics of pharmacies (both on a state and federal level)
- The names of different medications, the typical doses of those medications, what they do, and potential side effects
- Lab work may be required

Some of the shorter term programs and most associate's degree programs also give you the opportunity for experience in the field, called clinical experience.

AMERICAN SOCIETY OF HEALTH-SYSTEM PHARMACISTS

The American Society of Health-System Pharmacist also called the ASHSP, is a unique organization that helps train aspiring pharmacy technicians. It offers accredited programs with a minimum of 600 hours of instruction that will take you 15 weeks to complete. As of 2012, over 200 accredited programs existed under this umbrella. If you are interested in working for a retail drugstore chain, this could be an alternative to the more traditional types of schooling.

It is important to be aware of this particular organization because a handful of states require pharmacy technicians to complete training that is accredited by the organization.

CHAPTER 4. HOW MUCH DOES IT COST TO GO TO SCHOOL TO BECOME A PHARMACY TECHNICIAN?

This depends entirely on where you live and what kind of education you seek. There are courses online in addition to the more traditional types of schooling.

THE SHORT PATH

If you seek only to get certified, you will pay anywhere from $500 to $5,000. Here is a look at a few schools around the country, as well as online.

CAREERSTEP

The online program offered by Careerstep says the provide everything you need for less than $2,000 ($1,995 is the current price listed on their site). For this price, you get six full months to access everything you need to pass the certification. Six months is twice as long as they expect it to take. They say that the courses are designed to be completed in less than three months.

CALIFORNIA STATE UNIVERSITY

Since it is in the state with the highest paying rates for this career path, it is fitting to include information on a school that is within the state. The cost is also one of the lowest of the schools on this list at $999. It includes a course that should take you 50 hours to complete. Everything you need to prepare to take the PTCB exam is included in the cost, although it does not include the cost of the test.

EASTERN NEW MEXICO UNIVERSITY

Of the schools on this list, it has the lowest cost, depending on if you are in-state or out of state. If you live in New Mexico, the cost is approximately $700. If you attend and you live out-of-state, the cost is over $2,000. Additional fees costing more than $70 may apply. The courses are designed to be completed within three months.

OAKTON COMMUNITY COLLEGE

Located in the northeast in Illinois, this is one of the most expensive options. They also charge more for those who live outside of the district (not the state). If you live in the area, your tuition is around $1,200. If you live outside of the district, tuition is around $2,200. The cost for both covers the application and registration fees, tuition, fees for the labs, the cost of all necessary books, and the cost of graduation. The course is designed to be completed within 12 weeks.

ASHWORTH COLLEGE

Ashworth College is located in Norcross, Georgia offers one of the lowest prices, depending on how much you can afford at the time of your application. Because the course is online, you don't have to worry about additional costs for living in a different area. The cost ranges from just over $600 if you pay the full cost upfront to $749 if you pay monthly (the monthly cost can be as low as $49 per month). Unlike many schools, the cost does cover taking the exam.

FINDING A SCHOOL NEAR YOU

There are plenty of schools that offer students the option to go online. If you are self-disciplined and just need a teacher who can answer your questions, you can check out some of the schools mentioned above or do a quick search online. Make sure you take a look at the reviews and success rates of students so that you know that you are getting the information you need to get certified. You can also follow the steps for finding a traditional classroom listed below if you want a more focused list of schools.

If you prefer to have a classroom where you can focus and get lab experience, there are a couple of websites that can help you find a school near you.

- ASHP makes it easy to find a college no matter where you are located. They have a map on their website with a list of all traditional campuses where you can take classes for this career path.
  You can click on any of the schools near you, and the site takes you to a directory page with details and contact information for that school.
- Trade Schools, Colleges, and Universities is a great online resource for locating schools and seeing how those schools have performed. All you have to do is visit their website.

http://www.trade-schools.net/health-care/pharmacy-technician.asp

  - On the right side under the **Find a School** banner, enter your zip code.
  - For step 2, select if you want a school list of schools that have a **Campus**, **Online**, or **Both**. The site returns several pages of information based on the information you entered. If you only want schools with a campus, just click on **Campus**. If you want a more comprehensive list, click on **Both**.
  - Browse through the listed schools and decide which one you think is right for you.

It is always important to find the right school for the way you learn. If you learn better in a traditional setting, it is worth it to dig a little on these sites and select a school that has a high success rate for people who take the test. If you are comfortable going to school online, there are plenty of options as long as you do a bit of research before enrolling.

GETTING AN ASSOCIATE'S DEGREE

An associate's degree is a two-year degree, so you can expect to attend for the full duration if you want an associate's degree. Like any other degree, it is considerably more costly than preparing to be certified. If you plan to get a degree, plan to spend between $10,000 and $25,000. Given this much greater cost for schooling, you should only consider getting a degree if you are already certain it is the right field and are considering becoming a pharmacist. This will help move you on the right path if you need to have a higher salary but will need more time before you can work toward being a full pharmacist.

One more thing to keep in mind about getting an associate's degree is that you can spread it out over more than two years, depending on your schedule. If you have to work full time while attending school, you can find a school that can work with your schedule.

Since this book is dedicated to becoming a pharmacy technician, it does not cover most of the requirements and costs of getting the degree because that is part of the path to becoming a pharmacist. If that is your goal, the pharmacy technician is a stepping stone, and you likely won't need as many details to get started.

Check with your local community colleges and vocational schools to see what they offer regarding a degree and what you will need to do to advance once that is done.

COST FOR THE AMERICAN SOCIETY OF HEALTH-SYSTEM PHARMACISTS

The ASHSP offers a wide variety of classes for continuing education, whether you want to learn more about being a technician, a nurse, or another type of health care professional. They have specialty certifications and training programs to help you find success. The cost of these different programs varies based on what your primary focus is. You can register for several of these courses, even if you are not a member, for the fee posted to their catalog.

http://elearning.ashp.org/catalog

Keep in mind that this information is in addition to what you need to know and does not supplement the courses offered by schools. Classes that come with a fee are cheap, though, either $10 or $20. You can check back regularly as they update the catalog for the latest information and things you may need to know after you become a pharmacy technician.

CHAPTER 5. WHAT IS THE BOARD EXAMINATION?

The Board Examination is the one offered by the Pharmacy Technician Certification Board. The exam is commonly referred to as the PTCE.

Many states require that all pharmacy technicians acquire this certification before they can begin work. Employers may have their own requirements, especially those that operate in multiple states. Make sure you research both what is required by your state and the company you want to work for if you have already decided on a particular employer.

WHAT IT IS

The test is the more basic of the two available tests for becoming a certified pharmacy technician. It has much laxer requirements and is considerably easier to pass than the other established certification program. Since there are no federal regulations on what is required by those who are looking to follow the career path, states are able to determine the minimum requirements. With demand on the rise, many states are opting to require this certification over the second certification or more formal training.

The reason why this exam was established was because there were no overarching guidelines for the position, but there are federal laws that govern what a person has to know to work in the industry. This test is a way to ensure that people have the same basic skills and knowledge to fulfill this role, regardless of what state they live in.

This not only helps states but if you plan to move, you can look at states that have the same or similar requirements. If you have already passed this particular exam, you won't have to dedicate additional time to getting a different certification.

A BRIEF HISTORY

You might be thinking that this is irrelevant information, but it isn't, and here's why.

The PTCB was created in 1995 by four organizations, and was joined by a fifth in 2001 (the last bulleted organization):

- American Pharmacists Association
- American Society of Health-System Pharmacists
- Illinois Council of Health-System Pharmacists
- Michigan Pharmacists Association
- National Association of Boards of Pharmacy

The goal was to develop a national standard for those who wanted to be pharmacy technicians, including certification to help people determine if someone had the necessary knowledge to join the profession. This is actually aligned with the way other health care professions operate.

There is no federal standard, so this was the first attempt and is the most widely recognized and required certification within the US.

In 2011, a study was started to redesign the exam and bring it up to current standards.

When you look up information online, you need to be aware that there is a lot more information about the previous test than the current one. Check the date of the information provided to verify that it details information about the test that has been used since November 1, 2013. Any information provided prior to this date is likely irrelevant now.

REQUIREMENTS AND COST

The exam was developed by a large number of experts in the field based on a thorough job analysis study that included people from all across the country. The study was completed during February 2012, and it served as the basis for the exam.

To be eligible to take the exam, the following are required:

- A high school education, including either a high school degree or a GED
- A background check that gives full disclosure of any criminal actions and State Board of Pharmacy licensure or registration
- A check to ensure each candidate complies with the PTCB policies for certification

- That you have passed the Pharmacy Technician Certification Exam

You must apply to take the exam, which may be done online. The cost for the PTCE is $129 per test.

You can take the test three times in the event that you do not pass the first or second attempt. If you do not pass on your third try, you will need to petition the board to take it a fourth time.

DETAILS ABOUT THE TEST AND ITS DURATION

The PTCE is computer based and is offered at specific locations across the country. Here are the details for what you can expect when you sit down to take the exam.

- The test is multiple choice.
- Every question includes four answers, of which only one is correct (or in some cases is the best choice).
- Each test includes 90 questions, 10 of which do not count toward your score.
- The 10 questions that do not count toward your score are mixed in with the questions that do count. You will not know which ones are the unscored questions when you take the exam.

You need to plan for the test to last a full two hours. Of those two hours, ten minutes are dedicated to parts of the exam. This means that you have one hour and 50 minutes to complete all 90 questions.

The other ten minutes provide you with a brief tutorial to help you get started and a survey for you to provide information once you complete the exam.

WHAT IS COVERED

With so many experts involved, the test covers a wide range of possible job-related tasks. The following is a breakdown of the different areas you can expect to see on your test.

- The medication order entry and fill process constitute the largest percentage of possible content knowledge at 17.50%.
- The next largest required content knowledge is pharmacology for technicians, which has a PTCE content of 13.75%.
- Both pharmacy law and regulations and medication safety have a 12.50% content rating.
- Pharmacy information system usage and application has the next largest percentage at 10%.
- The next three areas that you need to know are sterile and non-sterile compounding, pharmacy inventory management, and pharmacy billing and reimbursement, all of which constitute 8.75% a piece.

- The last thing you need to know to take the exam is pharmacy quality assurance, which constitutes 7.5% of the PTCE content.

Be aware that the questions are not asked in any particular order, so you should not go into the exam expecting the questions to follow the order above, the order addressed in your course, or the order of practice tests you took prior to the exam.

If you would like more details on exactly what you can expect to be covered, the PTCB has created a guide that breaks down each of the above sections and details of what you need to know. It is in Appendix C of the guide.

With as much material as is covered by the exam, 90 questions may seem like too few. However, you will need to spend time studying to ensure you know the answers to the questions asked.

PASSING THE EXAM

The following is provided on the PTCB site to help you understand how your test will be scored:

The passing score and all candidate results are reported as scaled scores. The passing scaled score for the update PTCE is 1400, with a range of possible scores of 1000 to 16000. *Pharmacy Technician Certification Board*

This means that different scored questions have different weight toward your passing score. Some people miss more questions than others but still get a passing grade because the questions they missed were worth fewer points. The more complicated the problem, the more it is worth. It is safe to say that those involving math skills are more time consuming, meaning that most of the time math questions are going to be worth more.

Remember, there are also ten questions that are unscored (meaning they do not count toward your final score). This means you should focus on getting questions right, not on how many you can get right to pass. This encourages people to take a look at the exam from a different light.

APTER 6. HOW SHOULD I PREPARE FOR THE EXAM?

Ii ,ou pay to take classes, those will give you a lot of what you need to prepare. Make sure to follow the course outlines and information, especially practice tests and questions. This should help you pass the exam.

If you either don't have the time or the money to put toward classes and courses, there are plenty of available resources that can help you do very well on the test.

This chapter is really designed to help you become a pharmacy technician without having to spend hundreds or thousands of dollars.

If you learn better in a classroom, by all means, study the way that is best suited to the way you learn.

However, this is not for everyone, and it is not necessary if you have the discipline to study on your own. Between modern technology and the newness of the test (it has only been around for about two decades, so it is not nearly as well established as the exams for most other professions – save most high-tech careers), you can find everything you need for free online.

I'M PAYING FOR CLASSES ANYWAY

While it isn't necessary, this does show that you are dedicated and determined to get any additional advantage that you can. I

do not want to discourage you if you need structure and help to do well.

In most cases, the classes and courses will provide you with everything you need to pass.

If you still feel that you need more to do well, you can also use this chapter to take tests prepared by others to see if what you learned in your courses and classes stack up against what others are learning. If you do well on both the practice exams and questions from your paid class and the free exams, you have a much greater chance of doing well on the test.

Reinforcement is key in making sure you understand the concepts and ideas presented in the exam.

HOW MUCH TIME SHOULD I PUT TOWARD STUDYING?

Unfortunately, this is not a question that has a predictable answer. The answer depends entirely on you. If you are the kind of person who learns quickly and can retain a lot of information, you probably won't need to dedicate as much time to it as someone who needs to study something several times to retain it.

The important thing is to know how well you learn.

Whether you take a course or study on your own, you should always take a practice test or quiz over an area that you have just completed. After a couple of days, take a comprehensive quiz to see how much you have retained. This is the best way to ensure you are learning what you need to know.

DISCUSSION BOARDS

A quick word about discussion boards – they are one of the best ways of finding out how good a school is and determining if you are ready to take the test. The exam has changed since it first began, so you will need to be careful and only pay attention to discussion boards that have questions since late 2013. There are a lot of discussion boards, so it is best to look for discussion boards based on your specific questions instead of going to links.

Don't forget; you can post questions on these boards as well. If you had someone who was particularly helpful, make sure to thank them when you finish with the test. Also, give some encouragement to others. By helping to create a positive environment, you are supporting others. It is a growing field, and you will want to help as many people as possible to keep flexible hours. You never know. The person you help may end up being a coworker.

If you have specific questions, it helps to spend a bit of time seeing what other people have said. This can help you understand the scoring, what kinds of questions are the most common, and what areas had the most focus.

Make sure the discussion boards you visit cover the new exam questions as it was changed in 2013.

There are still some discussion boards that talk about the older version of the test. Remember the new test grades scores at over 1,000. If you see a discussion talking about a score of 650 being a passing score, that is an old discussion and will not help you.

FREE OR INEXPENSIVE RESOURCES

There are a large number of free and very inexpensive resources available online to help you study. A simple Google search turns up a number of different sites, including discussion boards.

Now, a little bit about the free online resources and some good books to help you study. This section does not go into too much detail, but if you are interested in learning more, Chapter 10 provides a lot of detail about valuable resources.

ASHP RESOURCES

As mentioned in an earlier chapter, ASHP has a number of courses and guides for relatively cheap

($10 and $20 for most of them). However, there are a couple of freebies as well. Go to the ASHP site http://elearning.ashp.org/catalog and run a search for information on the pharmacy technician tag. This will pull up all of the latest guides and help the site has, as well as the cost for each item.

PEARSON

The Pearson VUE testing tutorial and practice exam gives you the same look and feel like the actual exam. You get a chance to see how the exam will look and feel so that you already know how to navigate it before exam day. It is free, but there are some requirements that go with it. Check out Chapter 10 for more information.

If you have a Mac, you won't be able to use this resource as it is only compatible with Windows.

PHARMACY TECH STUDIES

Pharmacy Tech Studies is a site dedicated to helping students in a wide range of areas, including becoming a pharmacy technician. It offers a free study guide to get you going and help you learn what you need to pass the first time.

http://www.ptcbpracticetest.com/pharmacy-technician-schools/

PTCB

Not surprisingly, one of the best resources for learning about the exam is provided by the PTCB. They have practice test, quizzes, and study guides to help you prepare. If you find that you want something more traditional because either you didn't perform well on the practice information or because you are still not prepared all the way, then go to their web page to help you find a school.

BOOKS AND OTHER RESOURCES

Books are a great alternative to taking classes. Here are a few books and sources that can give you the edge you need without the high cost of going back to school:

- Mosby's Review for the Pharmacy Technician Certification Examination will run you up to $55 although you can look for a used copy for less. At just under 400 pages, there is plenty of material to help you study for and pass the exam.
- PTCE-2015-2016 Edition covers all of the latest changes. It costs about $45 and is nearly 200 pages.
- Secrets of the PTCB Exam Study Guide includes not only secrets but practice questions to help you prepare. It is shorter than the other books (not even 150 pages) but has a lot of

valuable information in those pages and costs about $30.
- Flashcard Study System for the PTCB Exam cost about $40 for new cards.

You can go to a local bookstore to see if they have a copy of any of the books that you think will help. You can go online and purchase a book from somewhere like Amazon. You can even find some of these as e-books, so you don't have even to leave your home to get started.

THE DAY OF THE TEST

One of the most important things to remember before taking any test is to remain calm. The more anxious you are, the lower your score is likely to be.

Keep in mind that the test is easy enough that people can take the exam and pass without every taking a course or attending a class. It is a growing field, one that is growing too fast. Unlike other fields, they want to make sure you know everything that you need to know to ensure customers are satisfied and get healthy, but the board does not want to make the test impossible. It's not the Bar Exam or a Ph.D. dissertation. They need you every much as you need them.

Take a deep breath and think positive. If you have spent time studied and done well on the practice test, you shouldn't have anything to worry about.

Ultimately, the exam is only as difficult as you make it.

WHAT TO BRING

When you go to take the test, you will need to bring identification. Acceptable identification includes the following:

- Driver's license issued by the state
- Driving permit issued by the state
- Passport
- ID issued by any national government (federal or state)
- Military ID
- Permanent Resident Card (also known as a Green Card)
- US Department of Homeland Security-Issued Employment Authorization Card

Check out the guide (under the Exam Day, Identification Requirements) if you have questions about your current identification.

https://www.ptcb.org/get-certified/prepare#.WObqu_Z1qM8

It is also a good idea to review the Test Center Rules in the same section prior to the test day. That way you know what to expect before you get there.

CHAPTER 7. ARE THERE PRACTICE TESTS FOR THE BOARD EXAMS?

Just as there are a great number of resources to help you study, there are a lot of websites and books that give you the practice you need to be prepared for the test.

If you are taking classes, these are a great supplement to see how you perform using something other than what you school has prepared. It gives you an idea of the areas where you still need to study and feel confident about the ones that you know inside and out.

DEDICATED BOOKS

Sometimes you don't feel that you are ready to take the online practice tests. These books can help you take tests and notes so that you can feel more confident. Then once you feel ready, you can take the online tests to see what it will be like when it comes time to sit down at a computer and put your knowledge to the test.

- Pharmacy Technician Practice Exam Kit is a book that is all practice exam. It gives you real exam topics and full explanations of what you need to know to succeed.

- PTCB Exam Study Guide: Test Prep and Practice Questions for the Pharmacy Technician Certification Exam gives you almost 175 pages of focused questions that are similar to what you will see on the test. The price range for this book is between $40 and $60, depending on who you buy it from.
- PTCE – Pharmacy Technician Certification Exam Flashcard Book Online is an excellent resource if you want to study online, but prefer to use flashcards. With 400 cards and explanations about the answers, you can really get your money's worth for only $11.01. You can find it on Google Play, so you can even access them from your mobile device.

With a quick Google search, you can find a number of excellent books and other resources that will give you something to hold while you study. When you miss a question, you can go back through it and scribble some notes. Experts say that writing stuff down is one of the best ways to reinforce it. When you encounter a similar question during the exam, you are more likely to remember what the right answer is, or in the case of math questions how to derive the correct answer.

ONLINE RESOURCES

Before you go in to take the test, you should really take the time to practice the test with online resources. Many of the following sources actually strive to give you the same look, feel, and navigation used on the actual exam.

PEARSON

The Pearson VUE practice exam is the one that strives the most to give you the same environment as the test itself (minus the testing center). You will need to download software to take the tests. Make sure to review the requirements before you get started.

http://www.pearsonvue.com/athena/athena.asp

If you have a Mac, you won't be able to use this resource as it is only compatible with Windows.

Plan to take this test a day or two before the exam so that the experience is fresh on your mind when you head into the testing center.

PHARMACY TECH STUDIES

Pharmacy Tech Studies has more than just a study guide to help you prepare. Their practice test could be just what you need to see how much information you have retained after all of the time you spent studying. See where your strengths and weaknesses are so that you can focus your attention on the areas where you are most likely to trip up during the test.

http://www.ptcbpracticetest.com/pharmacy-technician-schools/

VARSITY TUTORS

The Varsity Tutors have created a number of completely free tests so that you can start practicing well in advance to better hone your knowledge. Whether you need more practice on math questions or another area, the site scores your test and tells you how you did. They also have a question of the day and flashcards if you want a little extra practice.

https://www.varsitytutors.com/example-ptcb-problems

PTCB

No resource is as dedicated to your success as the PTCB itself. They want to make sure that pharmacy technicians have the same minimum knowledge, no matter what state they are in. To make sure you are prepared to take the test, they have an entire area on their website put aside to test you and see what you have down pat and where you should spend a bit more time studying.

A SAMPLING OF PRACTICE QUESTIONS

This section gives you a short sampling of the kinds of questions you are likely to encounter. The source for these five questions are the two practice tests on the PTCB website with a few variations from the actual practice questions.

1. Can you define the abbreviation q.o.d.?

A. Twice a day

B. Every hour

C. Every day

D. Every other day

The correct answer is D –Every other day. Q.O.D is an acronym for the Latin phrase "quaque otra die."

2. What are the fluid drams in 1 fluid ounce of a compound?

A. 2

B. 4

C. 5

D. 8

The correct answer is D – 8. You will use this on the job, so if you get hands on experience before the exam, that may help you remember.

3. What is the name of the autoimmune disease that causes the thyroid to be overactive, resulting in excessive amounts of hormones?

A. HIV/Aids

B. Graves' Disease

C. Anemia

D. Lou Gehrig's Disease

The correct answer is B - Graves' Disease.

4. Which of the following type of drug is loratadine?

A. Antihistamine

B. Antitussive

C. Decongestant

D. Expectorant

The correct answer is A – Antihistamine. It is commonly used to help treat allergies.

5. Federal law requires that DEA forms be maintained for how many years?

A. 1 year

B. 1.5 years

C. 2 years

D. 10 years

The correct answer is C – 2 years. It is very important that you know the federal laws and regulations, so there are always a few questions that you will need to answer covering these topics.

CHAPTER 8. WHAT DO I NEED TO KNOW AFTER I TAKE THE TEST?

Once you have finally finished the test, you will probably have mixed emotions. It is a relief that you are done, but want to know what happens next.

HOW LONG DO I HAVE TO WAIT?

You will know how you did on the test as soon as you complete the test. This is one of the benefits of technology. However, it will take between one and three weeks before you get the official results and your final score. This is because the PTCB takes the time to make sure that all tests go through the quality assurance process before sending out results.

If you passed the test, you could download the official results as soon as they are available. The certification for the results will also be in the PTCBs system. If you want to hold the results in your hand, a wallet card and printed certificate are mailed to passing candidates within three weeks of passing the exam.

You will not need the hardcopy to get a job, but you do need the official results. Once you know you passed, you can start applying for jobs, but you will need the official results to be posted before you can start working.

RECERTIFICATION

One thing that you should know is that certification only lasts for two years. You have to complete the following steps to be recertified by the time the two years is up:

- It is required that all certified pharmacy technicians complete 20 hours of pharmacy-related continuing education. You can space this out over the entire two years, or you can wait and do it all at once. Know that one hour of the required 20 must be related to pharmacy law.
- Go into your PTCB account and enter the continuing education information as you complete your recertification time.
- Once you have completed your 20 hours, go back into your PTCB account and apply for your recertification.

In the event that you don't recertify, you will have one year to get your certification reinstated.

Be aware that you cannot carry over your continuing education hours into another recertification cycle. If you complete 23 hours in a two-year period, you cannot carry those extra three hours into the next recertification. Once you are recertified, the number of hours resets to zero for the next certification.

Here you can add a new chapter which can be a short one, but the heading should be "My Personal Recommendation."

MY PERSONAL EXPERIENCE

I know how difficult it can be getting started. After my initial excitement, I began to feel concerned that I wouldn't be able to do it because I faced the following problems:

- I was working two jobs and did not have a day off.
- With two kids, I had to dedicate some time to spending time with them, including helping them study for school
- I didn't have any extra money to pay for books, let alone classes.
- It was an area that I had never considered, and there were no obvious resources to get started.
- I didn't have any family or friends who were in the medical field.

Any one of those reasons seemed like enough cause to quit thinking about it and keep looking for a job that didn't require any additional learning. All five of those problems together made it seem almost impossible. But I had already been down the path of trying to make the best with what I had, and I was at a dead end now because of it.

It wasn't easy at first because I was starting from the very beginning, where I had always had at least some guidance before. Looking back, I should have gone back to the pharmacy and asked, but it didn't occur to me until much later.

Ultimately, time was my biggest problem. I didn't have a starting point, so I knew it was going to take me a couple of days to get everything together before I could even begin to learn about the career.

I know that the problems I faced are not unique. That there are many people who already have a lot on their plate and barely enough to make ends meets every month. It's one of the reasons I decided to write down what I did. So with all of these problems, I know that it may seem impossible.

It isn't impossible.

If I can do it, I know that almost anyone can. As a student, my grades were usually Cs. Passing the certification exam isn't like taking a test for school. You don't simply cram and then forget what you learn. What you learn is the foundation for what you will need to know once you begin working. It is all practical knowledge, so you won't have to wonder why you are wasting time conjugating verbs or learning the hypotenuse of a triangle.

What you need is to dedicate some of your free time and energy you have into study. If you have a little bit of money you can put towards it, that can be very helpful, but it isn't necessary if you really work hard.

MY TIME DEDICATION

It took me three days to understand of researching to understand what a pharmacy technician did and what I needed to do. A lot of discussion boards made me feel nervous because they talked about how difficult the test was. The people who said it was ridiculously easy made me feel like maybe I shouldn't even start because I knew it wasn't going to be a breeze as it had been for them.

Still, I had started. I already knew that I would get three chances to pass the test. I also knew that there was no time for school, even if I had wanted to. I didn't have an hour or two at a time to go to a class, even if I had the money.

I did, however, have between an hour or two every day broken up in 15 and 30-minute increments. I made sure that I always got at least an hour in every day. When I was waiting in line at the bank, I was studying. I woke up a little earlier in the morning to study 30 minutes before my daughters got up. After the first week and a half, I even realized that I could study at the same time as my daughters. It was actually a very memorable time sitting around the table studying together. I helped them with their homework; then they would quiz me on mine.

You just have to keep an open mind about finding the time to study. Turn off the television a half hour early or spend less time on your smartphone texting with others to make the time you need to study.

MY BUDGET

I really did not have a lot of extra money at the time, so I largely had to work with the free resources online. I did buy two notebooks for taking notes and studying. I also got a couple of good mechanical pencils because I didn't need to sharpen them.

The only other cost I had was the exam, which was $129. I did not opt to have the certificate printed, but you can for $25.

If you need a hardcopy though, you can check with your library to see if they have books you can check out. I did keep a notebook where I jotted down the things that I thought were the most important to study when I was away from my computer.

You can also check Amazon and eBay for used copies of books if you want to study on your own, but want a little more than what you can find online.

MY RESOURCES

I had three resources that I came to rely on rather heavily by the end.

- Pharmacy Technician Certification Board has all of the information I needed to learn about

- the career, what to study, and find other resources.
- Pharmacy Tech Study site had nearly everything I needed to prepare, including practice tests.

https://www.ptcb.org/resources/cpht-toolkit/state-regulations#.WObsZPZ1qM_

I did use a few other sites (and they are mentioned in Chapter 11), but these two are the ones I used the most often.

Because they both have practice tests, I was able to make sure that I had really learned the information covered. I was able to walk into the exam room feeling that I was well prepared, even though I had not taken classes.

MY EXPERIENCE WITH REGISTRATION

Keeping in mind that every state has different requirements, there may be some difference in what your registration is like.

For me, I contacted the Alabama Board of Pharmacy, and they helped walk me through the process. If you take a class, they can help you through registration. Otherwise, the PTCB website can help you set up and account and register.

MY TEST DAY

I made sure to have my identification and reviewed the test center rules before going in to take the exam.

The first five minutes were to help applicants navigate through the test. Then we had an hour and 50 minutes to complete the 90 questions. I had enough time to go back through some of my answers, but only by a couple of minutes. The last five minutes were part of the post-exam survey.

MY SUCCESS

I had known before I walked out of the exam room that I had passed. As part of my preparation, I knew that the initial results were not the official results. Those take between one and three weeks to process. Once my final results were published, potential employers were able to verify that I had passed.

From the day I learned about pharmacy technicians to the day I started my first job was less than three months. I accomplished it all through dedication and research. With only a small budget, I was still able to pass the test.

All of the resources I used and the way that I studied are laid out here to hopefully help you find the same success.

CHAPTER 9. FEDERAL & STATE LAWS

The federal government does not regulate the position of a pharmacy technician, but that does not mean that there aren't rules and regulations that apply. Pharmacy technicians are expected to be bound by the same laws that govern all of the industry, particularly those under the DEA.

States have far more rules, regulations, and laws that apply to the actual position. They also expect that pharmacy technicians will know both the federal and state laws that apply to this particular career.

This chapter is meant to help you navigate the difficult areas that are regulated by two different types of government.

APPLICABLE FEDERAL LAWS

Fortunately, nearly every site and school that helps you pass the exam takes into account the applicable federal laws you need to know. The following boils down what you need to know about the federal laws that are relevant to you if you decide to pursue a career as a pharmacy technician.

- H.I.P.A.A is a relatively new federal law that applies to every medical career, from vision to insurance to pharmacy to medical careers. As you are dealing with the customers regularly, you need to fully understand H.I.P.A.A. before you take the test. The primary focus of this law is customer privacy, so it is relatively easy to see why it is vital you understand how to protect your customers' privacy and information.

- O.B.R.A. applies to Medicaid patients and counseling with a licensed Pharmacist.
- The DEA has a plethora of things you have to know (that is why there are 200 practice questions specific to drugs on the PTCB website). They regulate numerous aspects, including things as mundane as how long files have to be maintained before they can be discarded, and what you have to do to discard these records.
- The FDA has a lot of rules as well, including information on new drug application and recalls. You will need to understand these as you will likely help the pharmacist when they apply.

While it is important to know about the different DEA and FDA regulations, H.I.P.A.A is going to be the one that you have to deal with on a daily basis. You will need to make sure you keep customer data confidential and secure at all times.

APPLICABLE STATE LAWS

This section could be an entire book on its own because every state has its own set of laws governing the career. While the rules and laws aren't as numerous as they are for pharmacists, you still need to spend time understanding the applicable laws and how you need to ensure you follow them once you start working.

The best resource for understanding the laws and regulations for your state is to go to the National Association of Boards of Pharmacy. The site has information on the website with the laws and regulations for your state, an email address if you have questions, and other contact information (such as phone number and address).

Over 20 states now require PTCE certification. Visit the PTCB's dedicated page to addressing the applicable laws.

WHY IT'S SO IMPORTANT

All work in the medical profession is strictly regulated, even for technicians. Because you spend all day around controlled substances, there are a lot of federal laws that have to be followed. These are included on the practice tests and the actual test. When you take the time to learn them, you will be better able to serve your customers and ensure that you don't make any basic mistakes that could have serious consequences.

As a medical professional, people are entrusting you to help them get better. The best way to do that is to understand the substances that you work with every day. Even though you are following the directions of the pharmacist and everything you do that involves working with these substances is supposed to be verified, it is a much safer process when you understand what the substances are, how to handle them, what they can do, and when they are needed.

Because state laws more tightly control your actual activities and abilities, you have to know them inside and out before your first day of work. If your state limits certain activities to the pharmacists, you need to know this. If you are asked to take on some of these responsibilities, you will need to know when you need to point out you aren't qualified.

You have an incredibly important job, which is why there are so many laws you need to know. Keep in mind that these regulations are there both for your protection and your customers, that way you will give it the necessary focus when you learn.

The certification process also treats this area with particular care. From the initial certification exam that includes several questions that pertain to laws and regulations to the recertification that requires at least one hour of dedicated time to staying current on laws, they seek to make sure you can ensure the safety and health of everyone involved.

CHAPTER 10. HOW DO I FIND THE BEST PAYING JOBS AND LAND ONE?

Once you have passed the exam (and celebrated the achievement), it's time to start reaping the benefits. If you are like a lot of those who get a certification though, you probably aren't sure where to begin. This chapter gives you some helpful tips and tricks to find the right position for your goals and current situation.

IF YOU ARE UP TO MOVING...

Monster.com recently ranked the top ten best and worst states for being a pharmacy technician.

According to the site, the following are the best states for this career path based on salary with Californians averaging $16.86 an hour and Rhode Islanders averaging $14.00 an hour:

1. California
2. Washington
3. Alaska
4. Hawaii
5. D.C.
6. Oregon
7. Nevada
8. Colorado
9. Utah
10. Rhode Island

The worst paying states were the following, with West Virginians earning $10.51 an hour to North Carolinians averaging $11.51 an hour.

1. West Virginia
2. Alabama
3. Arkansas
4. Delaware
5. Kentucky
6. Missouri
7. Oklahoma
8. Mississippi
9. Louisiana
10. North Carolina

If you are more interested in learning what states have the most available job openings, check out the article to see where the most jobs are versus the fewest.

In the event that you decide to move, this can help you decide where to go next.

BEST PAYING JOBS

All of those in the upper 10% of pharmacy technician salaries worked for the federal government. Not only do they pay top dollar, but you also get a lot more benefits. You are also more likely to get a steady salary instead of an hourly rate.

The second top paying employers are in the outpatient care centers and physician offices. You keep regular hours within the same timeframe as the office you work in. They are less likely to work late hours and require additional time. They are also more likely to give you decent benefits.

LANDING THESE DESIRABLE JOBS

Getting training and experience (usually done as part of a class or course), can significantly increase your chances of landing these jobs. When having a certification is not required, it can certainly be a determining factor in if you will get the job. If you take the time to get both certification and experience, you will significantly increase the number of interest employers have in your resume.

If you don't have experience, you can look into substituting volunteering experience to help. Hospitals and other facilitates frequently need help and may be willing to let you do something in or near the pharmacy as part of a volunteer position. You can learn a lot even if you aren't able to work with the medicines.

If you have experience working with customers in another position, make sure to highlight that on your resume. If you have the chance to do an internship with pharmacy technicians, that is even better. This will require planning ahead of passing your exam.

Once you get that call for the interview, you will want to make sure you have practiced interviewing. Take the time to research typical interview questions and the best ways to answer them. What potential employers will ask does vary based on where you live, so it is well worth it to find out what they were likely to focus on in their questioning.

Getting a position with the top paying employers will be far more difficult than the other positions because these positions are more competitive. You will need to make sure to start getting experience along with your certification if you want to stand out from the other candidates.

CHAPTER 11. WHAT ARE THE BEST RESOURCES?

Thanks to modern day technology, it is incredibly easy to learn everything you need to know about this highly rewarding career. All of the necessary resources are just a few clicks away. Using these sites, you can get started today on a new career path that is full of possibilities.

Your future is your own. Take this opportunity to find a career that is both rewarding and financially stable. You can go nearly anywhere in the medical profession from here.

Take that first step and see just how far you can go.

STATE SITES

There are two sites that can help you learn more about what you need to know about being a pharmacy technician anywhere within the US.

NATIONAL ASSOCIATION OF BOARDS OF PHARMACY

Visit http://www.nabp.net/boards-of-pharmacy, and you will quickly see exactly why this is one of our top resources. Not only is it well organized, but it also contains a wealth of information about all 50 states. If you have more questions, you can get the necessary contact information for your state's pharmacy experts.

PHARMACY TECHNICIANS CAREER GUIDE

This Pharmacy Technicians Career Guide is entirely dedicated to helping pharmacy technicians. From finding the right resources to seeing what your current state's requirements are, they have the basics of what you need to get going now.

STUDYING AND PREPARING FOR YOUR FUTURE

The following three sites are among the most beneficial of all the sites on the Internet. You are welcome to research other sites because everyone learns differently. These three sites will give you an excellent starting point to start branching out and getting the information you need to succeed.

PHARMACY TECH STUDY

From study guides to practice exams, the Pharmacy Tech Study site has everything you need to start studying for the exam. By the time the big test rolls around, you won't have to have spent a dime on school if you have dedicated time to studying on this site.

PEARSON VUE

Pearson Vue's main goal is to give you an authentic testing experience, short only the actual test center. By downloading the test, you can get familiar with all of the navigation and formats that you will need to know when you sit down for the real thing.

Take the time to check it out, read the requirements, and make sure you are ready to go when your exam date arrives.

PTCB

Of course, I've saved the best for last. No matter what your question, the PTCB sites has all of the answers you need. The following are just a few things that you will find on the site that make it something that you should not only visit but bookmark and return to several times a week as you study and prepare for the big exam day.

- If you are looking for test preparation, this page gives you a lot of details about what you should do and how to prepare for the test.
- Exam day tips is a treasure trove of information on what you need to do when exam day arrives. From what to bring to how early you should be to what you can expect when it is over, this page can walk you through the typical experience.

- If you are curious about state regulations, they can give you the basics, then point you to the right sites for more information.
- The PTCB Guidebook has a comprehensive look at everything you need to know, from scheduling your test to preparation to recertification. It is 52 pages covering nearly any question you have.
- It probably comes as no surprise that they have an FAQ page as well. Scroll through their lengthy list of questions they get on a regular basis and see if they address any question you have.

At the top left, notice they have a whole menu of other useful links and information. Take some time to browse the site. Whether you want more information on the career outlook, the code of conduct, or information on fees, this site is somewhere to spend a lot of time to get all of the information you need to help you decide if this is the career for you.

APPENDIX - PRACTICE TEST

To help you prepare here is a short practice test. Remember, the actual exam is 90 questions. This practice exam covers 40 questions and is designed to help you get a feel for what the exam is like. This should help you decide what approach is likely to work best for you.

Questions

1. What form is used to report a medication quality problem?
    A. MedWatch
    B. FDA Form 79
    C. AR Form
    D. DEA Form 222
2. CIII drugs can be refilled how many times?
    A. 0
    B. 1
    C. 2
    D. 5
3. If you have a 60 day supply for a Colace 100 mg capsule prescription, how many capsules fill the prescription?
    A. 10 capsules
    B. 75 capsules
    C. 100 capsules
    D. 120 capsules

4. PRN orders are given for medication that should be used on an(n) _____ basis in a hospital.
   A. daily
   B. as-needed
   C. hourly
   D. regular
5. The _____ Book tells pharmacy technicians if two drugs are equivalent
   A. White
   B. Black
   C. Green
   D. Orange
6. What is a drug idiosyncrasy?
   A. A unique response to a particular medication
   B. An expected response to a particular medication
   C. A planned response to a particular medication
   D. An unexpected response to a particular medication
7. Pharmacy technicians should always wash their hands using anti-microbial agents for no less than ______ before, throughout, and after every shift.
   A. 5 seconds
   B. 10 seconds
   C. 30 seconds
   D. 45 seconds

8. What is a solvent?
    A. The larger part of a solution
    B. The solution itself
    C. The active ingredient
    D. The smallest part of a solution
9. If a physician prescribes a 120 mg dose of Gentamycin, then a 40 mg/mL prescription should have ______ of Gentamycin.
    A. 1 mL
    B. 3 mL
    C. 5 mL
    D. 30 mL
10. How many ounces (oz) are in a pound (lb)?
    A. 16
    B. 8
    C. 4
    D. 2
11. An excessive amount of ______ activity in a person's brain causes epilepsy.
    A. electrical
    B. blood
    C. chemical
    D. hormonal
12. DynaCirc is part of which classification?
    A. Alpha blocker
    B. Beta blocker
    C. Calcium channel blocker
    D. Ace inhibitor
13. Inflammation of a patient's main air passages is part of which disease?
    A. Asthma
    B. Bronchitis
    C. Benign Prostatic Hypertrophy
    D. Lung Cancer

14. The last two numbers of the NDC number tell you what about the drug?
    A. Where it was manufactured
    B. The drug product
    C. Who manufactured the drug
    D. About the drug packaging
15. Carisoprodol's brand name is _____.
    A. Solu-Medrol
    B. Claritin
    C. Singulair
    D. Soma
16. The Poison Control Act of 1970 was created to do what?
    A. Prevent discrimination against employees with disabilities
    B. Reduce accidental poisoning in children
    C. Allow patients to select the pharmacy they want to use
    D. Ensure the health and safety of pharmacy employees
17. You should administer how many mL to a patient with a prescription for 90 mg dose of naproxen via a suspension that has 25 mg of naproxen per 10 mL?
    A. 36 mL
    B. 12 mL
    C. 15 mL
    D. 40 mL
18. Use a crash-cart for a code _____.
    A. Blue
    B. Red
    C. Black
    D. Green

19. The generic name for Risperdal is ______.
    A. Ranitidine
    B. Raloxifene
    C. Risperidone
    D. Risperdal is the generic name
20. A neonate is part of what age range?
    A. birth to 1 month
    B. 1 month to 6 months
    C. 1 month to 1 year
    D. 1 year to 5 years
21. A technician working in a pharmacy can use the __________ to locate storage requirements for a specific drug.
    A. Manufacturer invoice
    B. Taber's Medical Dictionary
    C. Davis' Drug Guide
    D. United States Pharmacopeia and National Formulary
22. You should _______ an augmentin suspension, and it will last for _______ days.
    A. Refrigerated, 2
    B. Stored at room temperature, 10
    C. Refrigerated, 10
    D. Stored at room temperature, 2
23. Which of the following is not part of the seven rights of medication?
    A. gender
    B. time
    C. routine
    D. drug

24. Once a drug is administered, the time it takes the body to start responding is called _______.
    A. Drug half-life
    B. Onset of action
    C. Platelet reaction time
    D. Plateau
25. A patient asks you, the pharmacy technician, if it will be alright to drink grapefruit juice. The prescription the patient is picking up is for Coumadin. You should _______.
    A. Tell the patient to contact the doctor who wrote the prescription.
    B. Tell the patient to contact their regular physician
    C. Tell the patient that grapefruit juice is contraindicated while the patient is taking Coumadin
    D. Tell the patient to ask the pharmacist
26. I.V. room countertops should be cleaned with what?
    A. 100% Isopropyl Alcohol
    B. 70% Isopropyl Alcohol
    C. Iodine
    D. A regular cleaner
27. ______ filters are required for laminar flow hoods.
    A. water
    B. humidifier
    C. HEPA
    D. double

28. A ______ scale is sensitive enough to measure between 650 mg and 120 g.

    A. Any scale
    B. Class A balance
    C. Class o balance
    D. Class B balance

29. Which Medicare Part covers prescriptions?

    A. Medicare Part A
    B. Medicare Part B
    C. Medicare Part C
    D. Medicare Part D

30. You need _____, _____, and _____ to bill a pharmacy claim.

    A. Patience insurance card, PCN, BIN
    B. Member ID number, Condor Code, BIN
    C. Member ID number, PCN, BIN
    D. Patience license, Condor Code, PCN

31. A patient should receive _____ mL if infused with 125mL/hr over the course of 7 hours.

    A. 313
    B. 450
    C. 875
    D. 975

32. A Type _____ laminar flow hood recycles both air and exhaust.

    A. A
    B. B1
    C. B2
    D. B3

33. The U.S. Social Security Act was signed into law in July 1965. It created national health insurance for people over 65 who have met certain conditions. What is that program called today?
    A. Medicaid
    B. Medicare
    C. Retiree health program
    D. Ameriplan
34. An IV runs for 4 hours at 10 gtt/min with a drop factor of 20 gtt/mL. The bag has a solution that is 750 mg of the dissolved active drug in 0.5 L of D5NS. The patient has received how much of the active drug in two hours?
    A. 15 mg
    B. 45 mg
    C. 90 mg
    D. 180 mg
35. Solutions are combined at a ratio of 3:1. How much of the two compounds do you need to make 200 mL of the mixture?
    A. 150 mL: 50 mL
    B. 90 mL: 50 mL
    C. 90 mL: 30 mL
    D. 125 mL: 75 mL
36. Insulin should be stored at temperatures between ______ and ______ degrees Fahrenheit.
    A. 10 and 15
    B. 30 and 35
    C. 33 and 35
    D. 35 and 40

37. The drug dosage the forms with solid particles that are dispersed, not dissolved, in a liquid?
    A. Suspension
    B. Suppository
    C. Syrup
    D. Tincture
38. The ______ Act was created to ensure most prescriptions have child safety caps.
    A. Controlled Substances Act
    B. Kefauver-Harris Act
    C. Poison Prevention Packaging Act of 1970
    D. Combat Methamphetamine Epidemic Act of 2001
39. Prescriptions for anxiety and depression usually include serotonin-specific reuptake inhibitors. Which of the following does not belong in this classification?
    A. Paroxetine
    B. Ranitidine
    C. Saline
    D. Fluoxetine
40. _____ cannot be refilled, so it always requires a new prescription.
    A. Tadalafil
    B. APAP with Codeine
    C. Diazepam
    D. Methylphenidate

ANSWERS

1. A
2. D
3. D
4. B
5. D
6. D
7. C
8. A
9. B
10. A
11. A
12. C
13. B
14. D
15. D
16. B
17. A
18. A
19. C
20. A
21. D
22. C
23. A
24. B
25. D
26. B
27. C
28. D
29. D
30. C
31. C

32. D
33. B
34. C
35. A
36. C
37. A
38. C
39. B
40. D

Made in the USA
Monee, IL
04 December 2019